Go to the

Ripe Fields

First!

Focusing Outreach on Receptive Peoples

By J. Douglas Gehman

Library of Congress
Control Number:

ISBN 0-9765168-0-2

First printing • January 2005

Additional copies of this book are available by mail. Send $8.00 each (tax and postage extra) to:

Globe Publishing
P.O. Box 3040
Pensacola, FL 32516-3040
850.453.3453
www.gme.org

Published by
J. Douglas Gehman

Globe Publishing

Table of Contents

Dedication

This book is respectfully dedicated to the memory of Donald A. McGavran. I studied his writings in the late 1980s as a student in C. Peter Wagner's Foundations of Church Growth class at Fuller Theological Seminary School of World Mission. Dr. McGavran was alive in those days, but I never had the privilege to meet him. His insights and discoveries about how people become open to the Christian message had a profound effect on my personal faith and the ministry to which I was called in Asia, the island nation of Sri Lanka in particular.

I and many Sri Lankan Christians owe him a great debt. If it were not for his influence on my life and ministry I may never have made the changes that ultimately resulted in perhaps thousands of Sri Lankan Tamils coming to know Jesus Christ as their Lord and Savior.

Introduction

Warning: The contents of this book are controversial!

Donald McGavran first published *The Bridges of God* in 1955 and introduced a new idea called "people group thinking." To the western world's individualistic world view, it was a shocking concept. Later, when he wrote *Understanding Church Growth* (1970) he rocked the Christian missionary world again with the suggestion that, in light of varying degrees of receptivity among people groups, perhaps we should preach the Gospel to some groups of people and ignore others. (Gasp!)

Edward R. Dayton came along in 1978 and proposed that people groups' openness to the Gospel could be plotted on a "Receptivity Scale." To the far left of the axis were highly resistant peoples and to the far right were highly receptive peoples. The indifferent ones were plotted in the middle.

Receptivity thinking has been controversial ever since. To opponents, it seems arrogant at best, and down right disobedient, to suggest that Christians should be sorting through unsaved people to pick out the "good" ones first.

This book is about picking out the good ones first. More accurately, the ready (i.e. harvestable) ones first. Frankly, I'm a big advocate of the idea. I don't disparage missionaries who like to preach the Gospel where persecution, rock throwing, death threats and general hostility to our message is the norm. On the contrary, I admire their courage. But from time to time, I also have to wonder about their wisdom. Preaching to crowds who ignore you is

5

perhaps even harder. In that case, you really don't know if the problem is their indifference or your methods!

For my part, if I have a choice in the matter, I would rather preach to a crowd that is interested and listening to me.

I've been involved in missions long enough to know that you can't immediately distinguish between the attentive ones and the rock throwers. Sometimes you have to get up on your soapbox and start preaching, and *then* you find out!

It seems reasonable that we should be able to identify generalized *groups* of hungry people. And with this knowledge, it is to those people we should bring our message. Frankly, I see no profit in continuing to argue with the hostiles when hungry people are standing nearby waiting to hear the Gospel.

Call it favoritism. Call it whatever you like. But, when we have the choice, I believe going to the hungry ones is fundamental obedience to Jesus' command to make disciples. It is an essential part of what McGavran calls a "harvest theology," meaning we preach the Gospel expecting people to believe in and receive Jesus Christ! When they don't, we move on.

The idea of *strategic favoritism* is the essence of this book. In Sri Lanka, I proved this approach works. We made the decision to work among receptive peoples (whom we had identified as such through several years of mixed-results ministry) and it bore incredible fruit. When we turned away from the indifferent and hostile crowds to focus our attention on the Indian Tamils on the bucolic tea estates of that island nation's hill country, we walked right into the middle of a harvest field! In less than ten years we planted 30 churches and saw thousands receive Jesus Christ and become active members of those new congregations.

It was time well spent and I have no regrets. While we worked among the harvestable crowd, we prayed for the hostile and indifferent ones, asking God to change their hearts about Jesus.

Donald McGavran suggests we "hold non-receptive fields lightly." In the meantime, he advocates that missionaries focus resources on bringing in the harvest among receptive peoples.

My prayer is that God will grant you new insights into the harvestable people on your mission field. As you labor where He has placed you, may you find the harvest-ready people He has prepared! And may your reaping be bountiful for the glory of Jesus Christ!

Acknowledgements

This book has been a work in progress for nearly ten years. Honestly, it sat neglected in unprinted computer files for a long time while I busied myself with the routine work of missions administration.

I am deeply indebted to a number of people who helped me (finally) finish writing, editing and polishing this book for the printer.

My wife, Beth, lovingly but steadily prodded me to "get that book to the publisher!" My good friend, Dave Barnes, pushed me in the same way, and contributed his valuable time to read the finished manuscript and offer helpful advice. And my Media Department producer and editor, Lisa Hutcheson, gave the book a final look through, offering finishing touches.

Finally, this book would not have been written if it were not for dedication and love of the missionaries and national leaders who labored with me in Sri Lanka among a precious and harvestable people. Whatever I claim to have done in this book was done only with their help. It was a team effort all the way. I am deeply indebted to them for what we learned, what we accomplished with God's help, and what I am now able to relate to you the reader on these pages.

ONE

What is the Harvest?

Jesus said, *"Do you not say, 'Four months more and then the harvest?' I tell you, open your eyes and look at the fields! They are ripe for harvest."* (John 4:35 NIV)

His other famous statement about harvest is, *"The harvest is plentiful but the workers are few. Ask the Lord of the harvest, therefore, to send out workers into his harvest field."* (Matt. 9:37-38)

What, or rather who, is this harvest to which Jesus is referring?

Before we can answer this question, we must first consider his audience, the people he was talking to at the time. Jesus frequently illustrated His messages with analogies drawn from the agriculture-based economy of His day. Harvest was an effective metaphor, because many in Jesus' audience worked the land for a living. His parables, deliberately made relevant for His hearers, were stories about sowers, seeds, fields, weeds, laborers, grain, barns, and the harvest. The terms were commonly used and the meanings were very clear. Harvest was an ordinary word with a precise meaning.

Webster's Dictionary defines harvest as "the time of the year when grain, fruit, vegetables, etc. are reaped and gathered in." Harvest is a basic vocational term. Unfortunately, today most westernized Christians no longer live on the farm and do not connect meaningfully with the term and therefore miss some important implications of Jesus' analogy.

Agricultural words such as the kind Jesus used have very little relevance to our daily lives. In fact, for most suburban Christians, harvest is a religious word, a term we only hear in church! Perhaps a business term like "marketing opportunity," while not as poignant, would be more appropriate for western Christianity because it more clearly communicates the harvest meanings of timeliness, potential, and urgency.

Because of the disparity between the terms used by Jesus in scripture and their meanings in the minds of today's Christians, harvest today has come to mean something else. For most of today's Christians, harvest means *"the whole world of unsaved people at all times, whoever they are and wherever they live."*

Broadly speaking, the definition works. In evangelistic terms all who do not know Jesus Christ are the focus of God's redemptive purpose and are therefore a part of "the harvest." The Christian hope, indeed the very desire of God Himself, is that

everyone will one day hear and accept the facts and implications of the Gospel (1 Timothy 2:4). But practically speaking, like a farmer's fields that ripen at different times and seasons, some people are now more open than others to receive Jesus Christ.

When Jesus said, "Look at the fields! They are ready for harvest," He was certainly challenging his disciples to care about lost humanity. But He was equally challenging them to discern those who were ready for His message. The context of the passage makes this clear. Jesus had just concluded an important conversation with a Samaritan woman. The context indicates that Jesus' "harvest" focus at that moment was the people of Samaria. He observed that they, like a harvest field, were ripe, ready for reaping.

Jesus obviously noted the woman's enthusiastic reception of His message and her subsequent witness to her community. "The simple beauty of this language is only surpassed by the glow of holy emotion in the Redeemer's own soul which it expresses. It refers to the ripeness of these Sycharites for accession to Him, and the joy of this great Lord of the reapers over the anticipated ingathering." (Jamieson 1961:1034)

In *Understanding Church Growth* Donald A. McGavran relates the story of Baptist missionary John Clough, who in 1865 went with his wife to Nellore on the eastern coast of India. For twenty five years prior to their arrival the American Baptists had labored among the upper caste people of the area and had succeeded in winning fewer than a hundred converts. After learning the language,

GO TO THE RIPE FIELDS FIRST!

Clough and his wife, in a move that broke with conventional wisdom, decided that God was calling them to reach out to the Madigas (Untouchables) who were known to be responsive to the Christian message but had been bypassed "lest their baptism make it still more difficult for caste Hindus to become Christians." (McGavran 1980:11)

The Cloughs moved to Ongole and began baptizing a number of very enthusiastic Madiga leaders. "By 1869, hundreds were being added to the Lord." (McGavran 1980:11) In a remarkable story of service, relief and development ministry during a famine that struck the area, and bold decisions to accept and baptize Madigas as Christians, by 1878, only thirteen years later, John Clough and his wife had witnessed the ingathering of more than 12,000 souls among one of India's lowest castes.

In Nepal, a country of nearly twenty million and one of the world's most staunchly Hindu nations, Christianity has for decades struggled to survive. From its early openings to witness in 1951, by 1960 there were only 25 baptized believers in the entire nation. Over the next 25 years the church grew more rapidly and by 1985 25,000 people were baptized Christians. Even during this period of growth Christians, especially Christian leaders, were severely persecuted. Those who proselytized and those who converted to the Christian faith were subject to severe civil reprisals, including imprisonment and sometimes death. Foreign missionaries working in Nepal did so under great restrictions, serving mostly in medical, educational, and development capacities. Witnessing was extremely difficult and had to be done with great care. In 1990, however, political changes in the country brought new freedom to the Church in Nepal, nurtured without a doubt by the prevailing prayers of many Christians around the world. Suddenly believers were allowed to practice if not openly propagate their faith. By 1991 new estimates put the number of baptized believers at 50,000. By some counts that number was closer to 100,000. During that period, one missionary to Asia reported in a newsletter that "churches are springing up everywhere and it has been reported that entire villages have become Christians."

From 1987 to 1994 our missionary team worked with the one million "Indian Tamils" who live and work on Sri Lanka's more than 600 tea estates in the central hill country. The ancestors of these Tamil people originally migrated from South India for employment opportunities during British colonial days. They brought with them their Hindu faith and Tamil language, but remained a distinct people group, having never fully integrated with the Singhala majority nor with their 1.5 million "Sri Lankan Tamil" brethren who have lived on the island for over a thousand years.

We did not always work exclusively with the Indian Tamils. From 1984 to 1987 we traveled through-out the island conducting evangelistic crusades in cities and villages, preaching to everyone in English, Singhala, and Tamil. We soon observed a definite response pattern in our outreach. In any crusade location where tea estates were nearby, the Indian Tamils walked, often for great distances,

GO TO THE RIPE FIELDS FIRST!

from their simple homes in the hills to attend our meetings. While the town's people (most of whom were Singhalese) ignored the outreach attempts, the Indian Tamils consistently responded. Eventually we turned our attention totally on these people, and joined hands with some national leaders who desired to plant churches among them. From 1987 to 1994 we planted 28 churches among the Indian Tamils and baptized on average between 200 and 300 people per year!

Another example is the almost legendary growth of the Church in Korea. Since the first Protestant church was planted in 1884 Christianity has penetrated every aspect of Korean society. For example, forty percent of the capital city of Seoul is Christian. Ten of the world's largest congregations are in Korea. Full Gospel Central Church, in terms of its membership (at about 750,000), surpasses every other church by many thousands. Patrick Johnstone, in *Operation World*, reports that Korea also has the world's largest Presbyterian and Methodist congregations, and has hosted the largest evangelistic campaign (by Billy Graham in 1973), the largest Christian mobilization (CCC Explo '74, World Evangelization Crusade '80) with 2,700,000 attending one meeting. Korean Christians have also conducted the largest baptismal service since Pentecost (in the Army, which is now 65% Christian), Finally, Korea is the home of the world's largest theological seminaries (Johnstone 1993:337). One wonders what characteristics are present in Korean society that have made these people so responsive to the Christian message.

GO TO THE RIPE FIELDS FIRST!

The Apostle Simon Peter witnessed a great turning to the Lord of harvestable people during his ministry travels. In Acts 9 (v.32-35) Peter went to Lydda where, while visiting the saints there he found a paralyzed man named Aeneas. Through Peter's prayer and faith, Aeneas was instantly healed; the news of this miracle spread through-out the entire area. The scriptures record that "all those who live in Lydda and Sharon saw him and turned to the Lord."

Why do some people many respond to the Gospel while others, sometimes living in the same geographical area, are indifferent? Why were the Untouchables of Ongole more responsive than the upper castes? What factors were at work that suddenly made Nepal become a ripe harvest field, whereas before it was restrictive and resistant? Why did the so many people of Lydda and Sharon turn to the Lord as a result of one miracle? Why did the Indian Tamils of Sri Lanka walk for miles to hear a Gospel message when the townspeople nearby ignored the witness? Finally, what gave birth to the unprecedented expansion of the Church in Korea?

I believe there are specific reasons these things happen! I also believe we can discover and understand at least some of those reasons. And, armed with this information, we can work more strategically to bring in the harvest among people God has prepared!

Korea, for example, is one of the most ethnically homogeneous nations in the world, which allows communication between peoples to flow more smoothly than it might in more segmented societies.

GO TO THE RIPE FIELDS FIRST!

In a receptive environment like this the Gospel can spread rapidly and widely. Another factor possibly affecting receptivity is Korea's history of devastating wars and suffering which certainly has affected the culture's cooperate sense of security and need. Good relations with the United States during and since the Korean War may have helped early American missionary efforts, because the missionaries were viewed as friends of Korea. The ongoing threat from North Korea may be keeping urgent the Korean people's sense of need. And who can measure the amount of prayer and intercession that has gone up to the throne of God for this nation? Without a doubt Korea has been a nation in harvest, and the reaping has been phenomenal.

As we understand more fully what makes people "harvestable" and as we are able to identify specific harvestable people in the unreached world around us, we will then be empowered to more effectively reach them with the good news of Jesus Christ.

It is our responsibility, our commission, to go to the ripe field first! The following chapters will discuss how we can do just that.

Chapter

TWO

Why Focus on Receptive Fields?

To a farmer, harvest is about readiness, timeliness, and urgency. Every farmer plants and harvests regularly. A hopeful anxiety is a part of the whole farming cycle. It starts small but grows as harvest time approaches. Why? Because when the harvest is ripe, it must be brought in quickly! The harvest is ready, there is urgency in the air, and the work must be done quickly. Every other farm activity is side-lined by the work at harvest time. The harvest presents a window of opportunity and the farmer must get his crops harvested within it or they will be lost! He is therefore concerned about nothing else. He prays for good weather during the entire season, but especially during harvest time. He prepares his equipment, his labor force and his storage facilities for harvest time, because all of these things directly affect the quality, quantity and preservation of the yield.

When Jesus challenged his disciples to reach people, the harvest analogy was the illustration he chose. In his meaning, the harvest is receptive people who must be gathered into the fold. There are many fields (people), but the harvest is particularly those fields that are ripe.

When Jesus sent workers to the harvest fields (Matthew 10:1,2), and called his disciples to pray for workers to be sent to the harvest fields (Matthew 9:35-38), He had receptive people in mind.

It naturally follows that we too should take the Gospel first to receptive people. Priority should be given to people who are open to God. In the most practical of terms, they are the harvest. Other people can be monitored and reached when their time is right.

Jesus taught about harvest in a context of multitudes of hungry people. He ministered to thousands! He performed miracles and healed the sick and thousands followed him! It was in this context that He gave many of his teachings. Even when He took His disciples aside, He was preparing them for the same work. He promised they would do "greater works." He promised Peter that he would become a "fisher of men." The promise followed a poignant illustration. Thousands of fish were caught, so many that the nets were breaking and the boats were sinking! When Peter got back to shore he fell on his face and cried, "Depart from

GO TO THE RIPE FIELDS FIRST!

me for I am a sinful man!" Jesus replied, "Do not fear. From henceforth you will catch men." (Luke 5:8-11)

McGavran called this expectation for great things a "harvest theology." He contrasted it with a "search theology" which is primarily concerned with spreading the good news rather than gathering people in. Search theology assumes that the Christian's responsibility is complete after the Gospel is preached and the good news is put out to the listening public. Search theology leaves the results to God. The Christian's job is to witness to the truth, and having done that, the preacher is free from any further obligation to sinners.

Harvest theology, by contrast, assumes that our responsibility is not finished until disciples are made. Harvest theology expects that the harvesters will go, work *and* reap. They are expected to be *skillful* and *fruitful*. That extra responsibility demands a more careful approach to our work. God expects us to bring in His harvest!

We marvel as we read the Gospels and see the Lord of the harvest at work! We long for the same kind of response in the communities we are trying to reach. I believe Jesus' harvest model is our prototype; it is what we should expect from ministry, and it is basic to our faith in God and our call to be a Christian witness. But to have such effectiveness we must go to the harvest fields!

When God brings a field to harvest-time, through whatever series of events He chooses, the harvest becomes ripe and the workers can simply move in and reap. The wonder of the harvest is the magnitude of the fruit that is gathered for the glory of the Lord of the harvest.

The Apostle Paul gave God the glory for the harvest. We wrote to the church in Corinth, "I planted the seed, Apollos watered it, but God made it grow. So neither he who plants nor he who waters is anything, but only God, who makes things grow." (I Corinthians 3:6,7)

In my view, focusing on harvestable people is to honor God. Like an attentive worker, we work in our Lord's harvest fields, to bring in his crops. We go where the harvest is ripe. No farmer sends his workers into unripe fields. The workers always go where the crop is ready, and, being in the ripe fields, they are expected to bring in much for their labors.

We should be eager to learn about spiritual harvest, to study fields, and understand the processes God uses to bring people to readiness. Then, as we harvest, we should seek to understand all the agents—the persons, methods, styles, contexts, background, results, timing, etc.—that make harvesting even more effective. We should be continually growing in our understanding of how God works, what He is doing in the world and among people groups, to make them open to the Gospel.

The real marvel of every spiritual harvest is God doing what no man can do—that is, through the process Paul describes as "making things grow," He opens sinful hearts to His message.

The technical term that describes a people's harvest potential is *receptivity*. In Strategies for

GO TO THE RIPE FIELDS FIRST!

Church Growth C. Peter Wagner says this about receptivity and the harvest:

> . . . professional farmers evaluate everything they do on whether a particular activity contributes to the harvest. They prepare the ground and sow the seed not as an enjoyable end in itself, but as a step toward the harvest. They dig out weeds and build fences as protection against predators in order to increase the harvest. They walk through their fields in such a way as to not jeopardize the harvest. Then, when the crop is mature, they gather it in with great care in order to maximize the yield. (Wagner 1987:59)

Wagner lists four variables related to harvest and receptivity. He derives these from Jesus' parable of the sower in Matthew 13:1-23. The four variables are the sower, the climate, the seed, and the soil. The parable clearly stresses that the fertility of the soil is the one variable that primarily determines the quantity and quality of fruitfulness. The sower, the climate, and the seed quality all contribute to the process, but, all of those being equal, the parable emphasizes that in the end, it is the soil that most profoundly affects the crop yield at harvest time.

We can easily draw parallels to each of these four factors. The sower represents a minister of the Gospel and his/her giftings, character, and training. The seed represents the message of the Gospel and the means by which it is communicated. The climate represents external contextual factors, both local

21

and national (such as the economy, political and civil conditions, and environmental conditions such as geography, disasters, weather, etc.), that affect a people's attitude toward new ideas, particularly the Gospel message. And finally, the soil types represent the people themselves and their particular attitudes towards Christianity.

Those who disagree with my definition of the harvest might argue Jesus said the sower was sowing everywhere: on the road, in the weeds as well as on the good ground. The implication would then be that we should witness everywhere and to everyone. Current thought by many evangelicals assumes this position, and it is the basic motivation behind much of today's missionary efforts. Saturation evangelism, mass crusades, urban street witnessing, mass literature distribution programs, and broad deployment of missionaries to every possible field are examples of this philosophy. Much of the current emphasis on reaching unreached people groups is built upon the assumption that the harvest is everyone and all unreached people should therefore receive equal evangelistic attention.

At first glance, it is hard to argue this rationale. With the knowledge of a world lost without Christ, it is difficult to make a case against telling everyone about Jesus. Yet I don't believe wholesale sowing is implied in the parable of the sower. Nor is it the best use of God's resources. Every farmer who heard Jesus' teaching understood one crucial fact about planting: every sower does his best to sow seed on good soil! The fact that some seed falls on rocky soil or on the road side is purely incidental, and, I might add, unintentional. A farmer is making his best effort to sow on the good soil. Jesus used the analogy to illustrate the fact that there ARE indeed different responses to his message. He was not commanding his disciples to throw seed everywhere!

A sowing mindset, or a search theology, unfortunately encourages much random missionary activity. While sowing is necessary for harvest—this is an obvious principle—I do differ with the simplistic notion that sowing is the only factor for harvest. God's word is powerful, and it will not return to Him void, but to use this truth as a justification for thoughtless evangelism is irresponsible. God uses many other means to draw people to Himself. The Christian witness through the sowing the Word of God is certainly one of them. We must consider how the Lord of the harvest is already at work in people as we sow.

I believe that, like a good farmer, God "works the soil" in a variety of ways to prepare for the coming of the sower and for the harvest that will follow. The sower, his message, and the method he uses to communicate the message, is important.

Equally important are "soil" and "climate" conditions, which are people's circumstances and mindsets. Political, economic, and environmental factors can greatly affect how and when people become open to change, and to new ideas and beliefs. Specifically, their attitude toward Christianity can be profoundly affected by these external contextual factors. An earthquake, flood, war, or other cataclysmic event, or a subtle spiritual breakthrough secured through prevailing prayer, which is then followed by caring Christian witness, can sometimes open people's hearts more effectively than many years of "sowing" through preaching alone.

On February 4, 1976 Guatemala was rocked by a 7.5 earthquake. Over 22,000 people lost their lives and 74,000 were injured. Christians from all over the world stepped in to help with the recovery effort. In the following months, many new missions were started and in a few short years hundreds of churches were started all over the country, with tens of thousands of people coming to personal faith in Jesus Christ.

While it is outside the scope of this book to speculate on why God allows tragedy in the world, we can from the evidence of history, see how He uses such things to bring people to faith. The "Lord of the harvest" is constantly at work in His fields! Is it not wise, then, for the Christian worker to consider such factors when "looking on the fields?" Should they not seek to more fully understand their impact on people?

The field is the whole world (Mt. 13:38), but the harvest is that portion of the field that is ripe and ready. Some radical new thinking in missions is necessary if we are to embrace such an interpretation. For example, more research to identify harvest fields should be done. Missionaries should be more strategically deployed, and some re-deployment of missionaries—away from resistant fields to receptive fields—must be considered.

Thailand, for example, has had nearly 175 years of exposure to Christianity. The current level of missionary effort in this nation of 55 million is one of the highest in all Asia. Yet today evangelicals number only about 100,000 by the most generous estimates.

There are clear reasons for these statistics. Later I will show how Thailand is a relatively non-receptive field and has been so for a long time. While there are indications that receptivity is changing in the younger generation, and while missionaries to Asia are grateful for Thailand's openness to missionary work, should we not reflect about how many missionaries should be deployed there? Such questions should be a natural part of harvest discussion.

The Moslem block is receiving increased missionary attention, and it should because it represents one of the largest groups of unreached people today. Moslems as a whole have also traditionally been one of the most resistant groups. In places this is changing, but would not good stewardship require wise deployment of missionaries to Moslem peoples where receptivity is higher?

In *Understanding Church Growth*, Donald A. McGavran says we should "hold unreceptive fields lightly." In other words, the bulk of mission attention should be where the harvest potential is greatest, and only a "light" representation of mission work should be maintained among non-receptive peoples.

Christian missions can never hope to be fully obedient to the Great Commission to make disciples and plant churches "pante ta ethne" without consideration as to who is most ready to hear. With the time, financial and human resources that are available to God's people in any generation, it is incumbent upon missionary endeavor to make the most efficient use of those resources and to seek to bring the most return on God's investment.

Jesus cried, "The harvest is plentiful and the laborers are few!" This is a challenge to us! It is a reminder to His workers that there is a human resource deficit in missions. He commands us to pray about this problem! Wise use of human and other resources, and wise deployment of our limited workers to ripe fields is necessary.

In the next chapter, we will examine another scripture that supports a harvest-receptivity view of world evangelization.

Chapter

THREE

What About Resistant People?

Does the Bible say anything about resistant people? And, if so, what instructions does it give to us about how to respond to them?

The Book of Acts records many incidents where the first believers were persecuted for their faith, by people who were resisting the Gospel. Jesus too was frequently misunderstood, and treated abusively. Ultimately Jesus was killed for his message by people who would not receive Him!

We know by experience and by the testimony of Scripture, that being a witnessing Christian has its dangers. Jesus warned us to *expect* tribulation and persecution. He said we would be mocked, abused, and even put to death! He also told us how to respond to such treatment.

"But I tell you not to resist an evil person. But whoever slaps you on your right cheek, turn the other to him also." (Matt 5:39-40 NIV)

27

GO TO THE RIPE FIELDS FIRST!

Jesus commanded his disciples to "love your enemies," "pray for those who persecute you," and "rejoice when you are insulted because of me." He also instructed them to stand firm in their faith regardless of the consequences.

The Book of Acts records how the early church responded to persecution. On one occasion, Paul and Silas were beaten and thrown into prison for their witness in Philippi. That night they prayed and sang hymns (Acts 16:25). The next morning, when released and asked to leave, they refused and, standing on their Roman citizenship, demanded an apology from the authorities. (Acts 16: 35-40). Other passages record similar kinds of treatment and responses.

In both the Gospels and the Acts we see Jesus and His followers witnessing to both receptive and resistant people. For their preaching they were sometimes accepted and at other times rejected. In some places people rose up in anger; in others they accepted the message and were saved.

Always we see the early Christian believers standing firm in their faith and in their testimony for Jesus Christ. Also, except when they are imprisoned for their faith (and could *not* leave) we do not see the apostles lingering nearby their persecutors for long periods of time. Their response to resistance was to move on to the next place to preach the Gospel. When they did stay in one place for longer periods, there are compelling reasons for the decision.

Paul entered the synagogue and spoke boldly there for three months, arguing per-

28

suasively about the kingdom of God. But some of them became obstinate; they refused to believe and publicly maligned the Way. *So Paul left them.* (italics mine) He took the disciples with him and had discussions daily in the lecture hall of Tyrannus. This went on for two years, so that all the Jews and Greeks who lived in the province of Asia heard the word of the Lord. (Acts 19:8-10)

In this city (Ephesus), Paul left the resistant people after only three months and moved on to have a two-year discourse with another (more receptive) audience.

Matthew 10:14 is the strategic directive Jesus gives to workers who labor on unreceptive fields. This directive is an important part of Jesus' first commissioning speech to the twelve, and in it He tells his apostles, "And whoever will not receive you nor hear your words, when you depart from that house or city, shake off the dust from your feet."

Jesus was being clear about resistant people. "If they don't listen," He said, "Leave." There is more to Jesus' command than simply sparing his disciples wasted time and wasted breath. It has strategic importance. "Cleanse yourself from them!" He is saying. "Don't let their indifference, cynicism, or hatefulness infect you. Shake it off and move on!"

I believe there is a danger in prolonged ministry among unreceptive people. Their indifference, hostility, and faithlessness can infect our witness and plant within us the seeds of cynicism and negativism. How many Christians, churches, even missionaries do you know who have fallen prey to hard-heartedness around them?

The very essence of Christian witness *and* joy is the salvation of sinners! We and God experience His joy most powerfully through interaction with people who receive Jesus Christ. Our task, our obedience to God requires that we find these people!

In Matthew 10:14 Jesus commands us to NOT waste time with unreceptive people. There are receptive people nearby who need our witness. "Go and find them now!" Jesus is saying. "Shake off the dust of unreceptive people and move on!"

But how do we really know people are resistant? What are the determining factors? When we face resistance we may think the problem is our witnessing style or our presentation. How many times have we wondered whether people rejected our message because we didn't present the Gospel well?

Although it is not indicated in this text, using a new method to communicate the Gospel is sometimes effective. We must learn how to better communicate Christ, and one form of witness may indeed communicate better than another. Jesus certainly changed his style of witness for different people and situations. He sometimes preached to crowds and at other times He performed miracles and signs. He spoke to individuals about their faith, and His conversations were always specific to their need and situation. For example, His interaction with Nicodemus (John 3) and the woman at the well (John 4) were specific to each person's need.

Change of methods can improve response today as well. In Sri Lanka, for example, we discovered

that the minority Indian Tamils were very responsive to open air mass evangelistic campaigns. The
Singhalese people, however, who are the majority race in Sri Lanka, were mostly indifferent, and
sometimes even hostile, to open air preaching. We
learned over time that the Singhalese would accept
Christ more readily through a personal witness, in
a cell group and house meeting context.

What would cause this? Their recent national
history probably has something to do with the
Singhalese attitude toward public Christianity. Sri
Lanka is a nation born out of the ashes of the British
empire. It is the only land on earth that is the home of
the Singhalese people. They are extremely proud of
their ethnicity, their language and their Buddhism,
the national religion of the island. They are also
very sensitive to anything that appears connected
to their former colonizers, including "western" and
"European" Christianity. Public propagation of the
Gospel is simply too threatening to this sensitive
national identity.

This is not the case for Sri Lanka's Tamils, who
are a minority. Their traditional culture, language
and religious beliefs are less organized in Sri Lanka. While allowed and officially protected by law,
the Tamil culture and ideals are not represented
equally in the government. Tamils live every day
with such discrepancies. In 1980 their frustration
with the status quo was compounded when bla-
tantly discriminatory laws were passed by a newly
elected pro-Singhalese president. Tamil separatists
responded by murdering thirteen Singhalese sol-
diers in the northern Jaffna district. The island ex-

ploded in violent reprisals against the Tamil population. Over ten thousand people died in the race riots that followed. Civil turmoil and outright war has plagued the island since.

Open air preaching for Sri Lanka's Tamils is less threatening than it is for the Singhalese. It may actually be a boost as Christianity perhaps represents an alternative to the status quo of which they are suspicious. I don't mean to overly politicize Gospel preaching, but, people do in fact react to Christianity in part based upon the political climate of which they are a part. Whatever the reasons, we found open air preaching to be effective in reaching the Tamils.

My belief, however, is that the Tamil people are simply more receptive (perhaps *because* of the above environment) and therefore almost *any* method will be effective in reaching them. They are unhappy with their plight in life, and are hungry for change. Into such a void a message about God, love, hope and salvation comes to offer something new.

A simple change of methods does not necessarily improve receptivity in a resistant people group. McGavran's view was that the right methods are most important when reaching people at the middle of the receptivity axis, the indifferent ones. My experience seems to confirm this. However, we should always be willing to re-evaluate our methods when our work is not bringing people to the Savior. This demonstrates our desire to "be all things to all men" in order to win them to Christ. Changing fields should also be an option, if for no other reason than the fact that Jesus commanded it!

GO TO THE RIPE FIELDS FIRST!

Missionaries should not frivolously discard one method or program for another just because people are not immediately responding. Nor should they change their focus rashly. If a missionary has carefully prayed for, researched, and learned about a culture and people, and has labored to contextualize the Gospel (including learning the language) to reach them, he should then be willing to persevere. Learning a culture, and assimilating into a people group takes time, sensitivity and work. Field ministry and field studies are perhaps the only way to learn about people groups where no Christian witness has previously gone and no research has been done. Because understanding a particular culture precedes truly understanding how open to Jesus the people in that culture will be, more research work is needed among unreached people.

There are times when change becomes necessary. Jesus' command calls for action, and we therefore must be willing to leave an unreceptive people and go somewhere else. We do not disparage missionaries who patiently persevere in a difficult work among one people group over many years, but we must applaud those who leave resistant, unfruitful fields to follow the harvest. We must affirm and encourage such missionaries. To bravely extract themselves from a resistant field and target more receptive peoples is an act of courage that requires faith and sacrifice. Their refusal to remain in the safe and familiar environs of an adopted culture when that culture is not open to Jesus Christ, so that they can take the Gospel to another, more receptive people, deserves our respect. More of these kind of missionaries are needed!

For very good reasons, most missionaries find it difficult to leave an assigned field. First, they went to great effort and made big personal sacrifices to arrive on a particular field and to prepare themselves to serve. Sometimes they are assigned by a mission board and are expected to execute certain programs. They may have spent a lot of money and effort to settle into a particular culture and location. To now confront the possibility that their host people will not accept the Gospel message, and won't in any significant numbers turn to Jesus Christ, is simply an unthinkable possibility. The missionary declares, "I can't leave now, not after all this investment!" So, rather than move to a more receptive people, the missionary labors for years among an unreceptive people. He abandons his hopes and dreams for harvest, and settles for disappointing results.

A scenario like this is not uncommon in my experience with missionaries. It only further emphasizes the need to identify receptive peoples, if possible, in advance of missionary deployment.

Matthew 10:14 is not a license for harsh attitudes towards unresponsive people, nor does it permit poor methodology. It is a command to go and find receptive people. It is a command to expect fruitfulness, and accept nothing less!

Unreceptive people may become receptive in the future. If we know anything about church history we know that this is true. In the meantime, the Lord of the harvest directs His workers to receptive fields, while He works the "soil" preparing it for a future harvest. Matthew 10:14 releases us from obligation to an unreceptive field until that happens.

Jesus' words give me hope. Hope that receptive people can be, and indeed must be, found! This hope is the essence of Matthew 10:14. God intends us to be effective and fruitful in the harvest, and if we are not, then He commands us to move on until we are!

GO TO THE RIPE FIELDS FIRST!

Chapter

FOUR

Factors that Influence Receptivity

Donald McGavran did some of the first modern work on the subject of receptivity. In *Understanding Church Growth*, he summarizes his thoughts on the subject by asking the question, "To what degree is becoming a Christian a real option to members of this homogeneous unit?" (McGavran 1980:260) In other words, McGavran asks, "How much resistance or receptivity to Christianity exists in a particular people group?"

There are many reasons why a particular people group may be either resistant or receptive to the Gospel. Sociological causes, not only spiritual and theological ones, influence resistance or receptivity to the Christian message. McGavran asserts that for most of the world's Hindus, Buddhists, Confucianists, and Moslems, resistance to the Christian faith

> . . . does not arise primarily from theological considerations . . . Their resistance arises primarily from fear that 'becoming a Christian will separate me from my people' . . . The fact is that men and women, high and low, advanced and primitive, usually turn to Christian faith in numbers only when some way is found for them to become Christian without leaving their kith and kin (McGavran 1980:215).

In other words, people, being social and community beings, are very concerned what others in their group are doing and believing. This sociological element is one important factor that influences a people's receptivity.

The idea of group consciousness is not easily understood in the western world where individualism is a standard way of thinking. Western expressions of Christianity focus on the personal aspects of faith and have difficulty understanding how Paul's declaration to the Philippian jailor in Acts 16:31 can be genuinely true. "Believe in the Lord Jesus, and you will be saved-you and your household." In the same chapter we read that Lydia, the first believer in Philippi, accepted Paul's message and was baptized immediately, along with all the members of her household (16:15).

In the western mind, salvation is such a personal matter, that any influences on or consideration of another person, even in the immediate family, is purely incidental to conversion. Our worldview, and a stubborn cultural bias, simply does not allow us to accept that God actually works in *groups* of people at the same time even though the evidence of such things is clearly recorded in the Bible.

In the United States particularly, being concerned what your neighbors or family members might think about your decision to follow Jesus Christ is strongly discouraged. "All heads bowed and no one looking around" is the typical kind of instruction that comes from American pulpits. This of course supports our individualism and reinforces our belief that conversion is a fully personal matter. In western thinking, to go against the crowd, to stand up and walk to the front of an auditorium to become a follower of Jesus is a mark of true faith. We focus on verses that champion this kind of individualistic faith. The inverse, to be your brother's keeper, to consider the impact on family and friends, implies fear, compromise and weakness. In matters of faith, it is displeasing to God to care about the opinions of others. Western Christians are expected to follow Jesus Christ regardless of what their neighbors think!

People in the western world act independently in almost every area of life, not just in religion. Career choices, marriage partners, styles of dress, and almost every other decision in life is focused primarily upon a world view that worships personal choice, personal freedom, and the rights of the individual. We may consult others about life decisions, but ultimately nearly everyone expects us to make our own choices. The western world view insists that our personal choices and freedoms are "inalienable rights" that must constantly be guarded and honored.

The Declaration of Independence emphatically begins with "We hold these truths to be self-evident, that all men are created equal; that they are endowed by their Creator with inherent and inalienable rights; that among these, are life, liberty, and the pursuit of happiness . . ." While no one will argue the truth in this statement, the emphasis of individual rights over community responsibility is a dangerous trend in the United States. It is no wonder we have so many broken families and lonely people.

Such individualism is foreign and very odd to most non-western cultures. In many such societies individualistic thinking is considered very strange. It is associated with rebellion and socio-pathologies. Group consensus and respect for the status quo is much more important than an individual's personal freedoms and choices. The individual is expected to respect the group, accept the status quo, honor the family hierarchy, and submit to the civil authorities.

Scripturally, it is difficult to argue with such a position. These too are Christian attributes, because they value respect for authority, family, and the common good of the community.

"People consciousness" is McGavran's term to define a society whose members are very conscious of one another and of the cooperate responsibility. Such people "think of themselves as a separate tribe, caste, or class" and are very conscious of those distinctions. In *Understanding Church Growth* he elaborates the concept:

> The degree of people consciousness is an aspect of social structure which greatly influences when, how, and to what extent the Gospel will flow through that segment of the social order. Castes or tribes with high people consciousness will resist the Gospel primarily because to them becoming a Christian means "joining another people." They refuse Christ not for religious reasons, not because they love their sins, but precisely because they love their brethren (McGavran 1980:214).

This group consciousness is an important factor in a peoples' receptivity or resistance to the gospel. There are some people groups whose culture has such overt antagonism to Christianity that becoming a Christian is realistically impossible for the majority. Only a daring few will break with the ranks of their people to follow Jesus Christ. On the other hand, other people groups view Christianity more favorably and many of their numbers may embrace Jesus Christ if given the opportunity, especially if a number of leading people in the group decide Christianity is good.

Missiologists and Christian anthropologists have always been intrigued by the sometimes complex chain of events that influence change in a people group's attitude toward Christianity. A highly resistant group may become open to the Gospel as events occur that upset the infra-structure or psyche of the group. When these things happen, the group's normal cultural cohesiveness and hierarchy is changed in some way and the group then becomes open to outside influences.

Such events can be either cataclysmic or subtle. Wars, famines, natural disasters, and the like are examples of the types of major upheavals that can radically affect change in peoples. Christians obviously should not instigate revolutionary or cataclysmic events, but they should be available to help people, both in spiritual and humanitarian ways, when such events occur.

In Sri Lanka, the one million "Indian Tamils" who work primarily on the nation's tea estates, are Hindus who originally came from South India. They have for decades been moderately receptive to the Gospel. The reason for their receptivity I believe, is the result of a number of cataclysmic social events in their past. First, tens of thousands of these Indian Tamils migrated to Sri Lanka during the rule of the British Empire, They came to Sri Lanka to work on Britain's expanding tea plantations in the central hill country. Their departure from their homes in India, the disappointments they faced upon arrival in Sri Lanka, and the desperate conditions in which they were forced to live demoralized these normally staunchly Hindu people. Later, after Sri Lanka won its independence from Great Britain (in 1948), the island's Buddhist majority began instituting an increasingly nationalistic Buddhist, Singhalese political agenda that alienated the Tamil minority. Their loss of a homeland, their stateless, minority status in a foreign country, their desperate economic plight, and the discrimination imposed on them by a Singhala speaking, Buddhist majority, severed the Tamils from the protections and definitions of their cultural past.

The result? They have become receptive to new things. Into that void the Christian message was introduced. The Gospel came with a redemptive message of love, help, and hope from God Himself for their future as a people. Thousands readily accepted Jesus Christ as their new-found Savior.

In 1995, another ministry of which I am a part started a child feeding program in the mountains of Albania. For 500 years Albania has been a staunchly Muslim nation and has resisted every attempt by Christians to win them to Jesus Christ. In the mid-1990s Albania experienced a debilitating national scandal after the country's leaders, through a lottery system, defrauded the people out of millions of dollars worth of the citizens' money. Nationwide riots and chaos broke out and for a year almost complete anarchy reined.

When our ministry, which had started just prior to the riots, returned to Albania, they resumed a feeding program for the poor children in the village of Rodokal. The village leaders asked, "Must we convert to Christianity for you to feed our children?" The answer of course was no, but the leaders of the ministry asked that they be permitted to share their faith with the children and their parents at every meal. They were given this permission, and over the years that followed hundreds of families were won to Jesus Christ. Today there are two thriving churches in this mountain region and the ministry is touching over 5000 children and their families every week.

Anthropologists have long asserted that outsiders (i.e. missionaries) can never be the innovators in culture change. They can serve only as advocates of change. If changes are to be accepted and incorporated into a people group, that group and its leaders must accept the change and make the new beliefs or practices their own. Harvest theology and receptivity thinking simply tries to be more intentional and thoughtful in finding receptive people and helping them in that process.

Don Richardson's principle of "Concept Fulfillment" (Winter 1992:C-59) suggests that every culture has built in concepts that can be correlated to biblical truths. The missionary's job is to find those concepts and meaningful correlate them to the Gospel message. Concept fulfillment can help receptivity, by improving communication in an already open culture. Concept fulfillment, used as a communication tool, seeks to make the gospel relevant and favorable to a given people and make it easier for them to accept Christianity. Richardson' book "Peace Child" tells the story about how concept fulfillment worked in one jungle tribe.

In *Understanding Church Growth* (Chapter Thirteen, entitled "The Receptivity of Men and Societies") McGavran lists six "Common Causes for Fluctuation in Receptivity." He says: "Myriads of factors affect responsiveness; I cannot attempt to list them all. A few, however, are so common and influential that they should be set forth."

GO TO THE RIPE FIELDS FIRST!

(McGavran 1980:256) He lists 1) New settlements; 2) Returned travelers; 3) Conquests; 4) Nationalism; 5) Freedom from control; and 6) Acculturation, as causes for both increased receptivity and increased resistance, depending on many internal and external variables.

In their book *Planning Strategies for World Evangelization*, Revised Edition, Edward R. Dayton and David A. Fraser list five variables that relate to how peoples are receptive to the Christian faith:

1. *The degree to which a people is satisfied with its present fate in life.* If their current customs and religion give satisfactory answers, they will be unlikely to listen for another way of life.

2. *The degree to which the rest of their life is changing.* Research shows that new immigrants or people who have recently moved to a new community are more open to new ideas and ways. So too are minorities who are away from their normal communities. They are no longer surrounded by friends who support their traditional identity.

3. *The cultural sensitivity of the gospel presentation.* Most people resist having their culture taken away from them. When Christianity appears to require leaving one's traditional culture, there often is strong resistance. If they are giving up their old culture, then Christianity must ride that trend as well and offer a new cultural identity.

4. *The agent of Christian faith.* Because of cultural biases and prejudices, some people receive a more respectful hearing than others. A young, Western educated missionary may not be as well received as evangelists with very different characteristics.

5. *The relative fit between the gospel and the cultural patterns that are presently dominant in a people group.* A deeply rooted religious system that stands in opposition to Christianity will create strong resistance to evangelization. This is true also of groups whose occupation puts them on the margins of society: drug traffickers, thugs, and pimps/ prostitutes. They can be won to Christ. But their economic interests create a natural resistance that must be overcome (Dayton 1990:129,130).

Another factor that seems to influence receptivity has in recent years been the focus of increased study by evangelicals. The biblical subject of spiritual warfare, long a basic ministry tool of Pentecostal and Charismatic Christians, is now being evaluated in a new way. As a means to win people to Jesus Christ, to release God's redemptive power, and break demonic strongholds, prayer and spiritual warfare has in recent decades been embraced by a much wider section of the Church.

The premise of spiritual warfare, as it relates to the subject of receptivity, is that people are resistant to God and the Gospel, not only because of cultural or social factors, but because demonic forces control and influence them. Demonic powers oppose the work of the Holy Spirit, and blind people's minds and hearts. The only way to combat such resistance is through spiritual battle, waged not with techniques in sociology or anthropology, but through intercessory prayer, using the name of Jesus Christ.

Jesus' healing ministry and His regular confrontation of demonic powers, as well as the early church's experience in Acts, particularly the apostle Paul's "power encounter" or "spiritual encounter" ministry (Acts 13:6-12; 19:11-20), and Peter's healing of Aeneas in Lydda (Acts 9:32-35), are prime examples of the effectiveness of spiritual warfare.

The late Alan R. Tippett, missionary to the Solomon Islands and a leading authority on animism until his death in 1988, has written about the "spiritual encounter" as a powerful tool to convince animists of the power of Jesus Christ. In the 1980s, at Fuller Theological Seminary School of World Mission, Pastor John Wimber and Dr. C. Peter Wagner did extensive research into and writing about the dynamics of prayer and spiritual warfare.

I come from a background that has utilized these powerful spiritual weapons on the mission field. I too believe spiritual warfare affects how people respond to the Gospel. Any real attempt to influence a people with the Gospel of Jesus Christ must be done with a serious measure of prayer and sensitivity to the invisible realms of spiritual activity.

One compelling dynamic of spiritual warfare is the fact that it empowers Christians to actually participate in the process of people becoming receptive to Jesus Christ. Unlike other factors, like wars, natural disasters, etc. (that are not controllable by individual Christians or the Church), spiritual warfare is pro-active.

In a 1994 telephone conversation, Peter Wagner related to me that this pro-active element is precisely the reason Church Growth analysts became interested in spiritual warfare. Their investigation was essentially asking, "To what degree can spiritual warfare, as a Christian exercise, affect the receptivity of unreached people?" By the practice of intercession, and prayerful "binding of the strong man," can Christians increase receptivity which would not otherwise be possible? According to Wagner, studies such as these were being done, and the data, while sketchy, was encouraging.

Spiritual Warfare should never be placed in competition with or as an alternative to the social causes of receptivity, conversion and cultural change. Both spiritual and human factors are an important part of how God works with people and causes them to become receptive to Christianity.

During more than 25 years in ministry I have seen the Church ignore one and then the other. The Pentecostal and Charismatic tradition has been guilty of negligence in both understanding and utilizing the social and human elements of evangelism and communicating the Gospel. Pentecostals have frequently overemphasized spiritual tools and have paid too little attention to social, cultural, and environmental considerations.

GO TO THE RIPE FIELDS FIRST!

Alternatively, the non-Pentecostal sector of evangelicalism has, in the past, overemphasized cultural and social issues and not given enough consideration to the spiritual forces that are at work behind the scenes in every missionary setting. The healing and miraculous elements of Christian faith have in times past had little part of their outreach.

Both sociological and spiritual factors are essential to witness. Neither should be neglected. Thankfully, in recent decades the Church has been growing in the use of both important aspects of receptivity!

Whether by sociological, political, environmental, cosmological or spiritual means, God is at work in the fields of the world! He is the Lord of the harvest, and He is watching over His fields, bringing them to their harvest time. Not all will come, not all will be reaped, but God is nudging them toward Himself. Like a great Aristocrat He is manipulating human history, and is influencing the hearts and minds of world leaders. He governs the complex workings of planet earth—the geographical, meteorological and cosmological elements—to bring about His purposes. Our responsibility as workers in His fields, is to be attentive to what He is doing and to participate—wisely and diligently—in the work He prepares for us to do.

GO TO THE RIPE FIELDS FIRST!

Chapter

Tools for Measuring Receptivity

Over the past several decades a number of missiologists have worked on developing tools to measure receptivity, the fore-runner of whom was Donald McGavran. In Chapter 13 of *Understanding Church Growth*, McGavran writes a section entitled "The Bearing of Receptivity on Outreach" and says:

> I have been analyzing receptivity not as an intellectual exercise but to obtain light on the complex process of church growth. The correct response to this chapter is not mental pleasure in understanding how receptivity fluctuates, but rather joy that through knowing these variations we may be more faithful in the discharge of our stewardship and commission.
>
> Ministers and missionaries often ask, Are the factors which create receptivity measur-

able, so that with proper techniques of appraisal we can know that such and such a population is ready for the Gospel or is on the way to becoming ready? One keen churchman asked, Could measurements be fed into a computer so that the Church would know exactly the degree of receptivity and whether it was increasing or decreasing? The answers to these questions are "in the distant affirmative." Someday this will become possible. Indeed, today a trained observer can judge with a fair degree of accuracy that a given homogeneous unit is in a state where its members will welcome change. But in practice, rather than carry on an elaborate program of measurement, the Church or mission has at hand a quicker and more reliable method of ascertaining receptivity.

Are groups of persons becoming Christians? As Jesus Christ is proclaimed to this population and His obedient servants witness to Him, do individuals, families, and chains of families come to faith in Him? Are churches being formed? Is any denomination working in similar peoples planting self-propagating congregations? If the answers are in the affirmative, the homogeneous unit concerned is receptive.

Once receptivity is proved in any one segment of society, it is reasonable to assume that other similar segments will prove receptive. Evangelism can be and ought to be directed to responsive persons, groups, and segments of society (McGavran 1980: 257).

GO TO THE RIPE FIELDS FIRST!

McGavran believed that the primary way to determine whether or not a people group is receptive is to *observe* what is happening within the group in terms of their response to the Gospel. In other words, field testing is one of the best methods to determine receptivity of a people. In my view, this is the one great justification for wide, if not massive, deployment of missionaries to every unreached people. In this position they can observe and "test" harvest potential.

Because every mission deals with limitations in their missionary force, my suggestion would be that when surveying unreached peoples groups for missionary deployment, one should list those groups that have recently experienced one of the upheavals or other factors on McGavran's list that affect receptivity. Those groups will probably be more receptive.

Missionary work in the former Soviet Union in the late 1980s and early 1990s is a good example of responsive deployment to a receptive field. Formerly closed to all missionary work, when the Eastern block began to dismantle communism and opened its doors to the outside world, Christian missionaries quickly embraced the opportunity and found a field so receptive that in many cases they could not manage the magnitude of response. While there were problems with the new openness, but no one can dispute that the original openness was phenomenal, and the church anticipated it in advance.

Time will tell whether the December 26, 2004 earthquake and resulting tsunami in Asia that took the lives of over 150,000 people and devastated the coastal areas of Sumatra, Indonesia, Sri Lanka,

GO TO THE RIPE FIELDS FIRST!

South India, the Maldives and other places will open doors to Christian witness in many of these formerly resistant fields. As Christians step in to provide humanitarian aid and offer comfort in Jesus' name they may find themselves serving people who are newly open to the claims of the Gospel.

Peter Wagner, in his seminary course, Foundations for Church Growth, at Fuller Theological Seminary School of World Mission, has developed a model for understanding receptivity theory. His model includes four steps to evaluate receptivity in a given field. The steps are: (1) Develop people vision (i.e. learn to see people in groups); (2) Identify your church's homogeneous unit(s); (3) Identify your target community's homogeneous unit(s); and, as best you can, (4) Plot each homogeneous unit on a Resistance—Receptivity Scale.

The Resistance—Receptivity Scale

-5 -4	-3 -2	1 0 +1	+2 +3	+4 +5
Strongly Opposed	Somewhat Opposed	Indifferent	Somewhat Favorable	Strongly Favorable

The Resistance—Receptivity Scale was developed by Edward R. Dayton in 1978 (Dayton 1978:9) as a tool for visualizing and charting receptivity. Basically the Scale is a numbered axis with zero marking the center point. Positive points 1 to 5 proceed to the right on the axis and negative points 1 to 5 proceed to the left. The zero marks people groups that are basically indifferent to the

GO TO THE RIPE FIELDS FIRST!

Gospel. On an increasing scale, proceeding outward in both directions from the center, the right grades those who are receptive and the left grades those who are resistant. The axis is meant to encourage thoughtful reflection about receptivity or resistance of specific people groups.

The R/R Scale assumes that, once we have determined a level of receptivity or resistance, we should, in obedience to God, focus the bulk of our time, attention, resources, and personnel on receptive peoples, or those to the far right on the axis.

It is interesting to note that Wagner and McGavran assert that at the mid-range of the axis good methodology is of utmost importance. On the right end of the scale, highly receptive peoples will be won easily, even with poor methods. On the left end, highly resistant peoples will rarely be won despite even the best approach. But in the middle range, good methodology can mean the difference between effective and ineffective evangelism.

McGavran's hope, that more accurate methods for the prediction and determination of receptive people's will some day be developed, may be coming true. In his 1993 book *Penetrating Missions' Final Frontiers*, in Chapter Six entitled "The Basic Strategy for Reaching the Unreached," Tetsunao Yamamori, President of Food for the Hungry, developed a tool to help catalog receptive people. He called this tool the "Openness Index" and bases it upon four sub-indices: (1) the Hospitality Index; (2) the Conversion Index; (3) the Receptivity Index; and (4) the Development Index.

GO TO THE RIPE FIELDS FIRST!

The *Hospitality Index* refers to the degree to which the leaders—of a country, or a cultural group within a country, or of a people group—are hospitable to Christianity. It refers especially to the quantity and severity of social (or governmental) sanctions placed upon gospel witness. . . .

The *Conversion Index* refers to the percentage of people within a given population who would identify themselves as Christians, especially in a safe environment where no persecution would be expected. . . .

The *Receptivity Index* gauges how much the members of a particular population or people group are receptive to the gospel. Unlike the hospitality index, which refers to the relative absence of group or governmental sanctions on Christian witness and activity, the receptivity index reflects the relative openness to gospel witness among *individuals* within the group. . . .

The *Development Index* seeks to measure the conditions of physical need in a target group and, more importantly, to measure whether there is a genuine need for physical relief and development assistance from outside sources (Yamamori 1993:86). Each of these indices are laid out in chart form in Yamamori's book.

To use the Openness Index for a particular people group, a number, from 1 (lowest) to 10 (highest) is charted for each sub-index.

> The maximum imaginable level of hospitality, conversion, people's receptivity and need for development would be scored as a

ten, moderate levels would be five, and so on. As specific countries and groups are evaluated, only a handful would be expected to rate at the lowest levels in all four categories. In most cases, even in relatively restricted-access countries, one would expect to see a divergence in these scales. (Yamamori 1993:87)

With these tools Yamamori has taken receptivity analysis to new levels.

McGavran suggested that one of the problems missiologists face in determining receptivity is the lack of field research. Because little or no work has been done among unreached people, there is very little data upon which to base any receptivity analysis. Yamamori echoes this thought in *Penetrating Missions' Final Frontier*s:

It will often be difficult and somewhat subjective to establish openness scale ratings for a given country or people group, especially since in most unreached groups it would be impossible to survey the group members and their leadership. In such cases, missionaries or Special Envoys (i.e. neo-tentmakers—notation mine) who have worked with these populations could be surveyed and asked to give their best guesses about the ratings for each of the four scales. Even though the final figures will not have a high level of demonstrable reliability, these "guestimated" ratings will still be quite helpful as a way of guiding us to the most appropriate mission strategies (Yamamori 1993:87).

In my opinion, these limitations notwithstanding, Yamamori's Openness Index is one of the most innovative tools for analyzing receptivity that has been developed in more than ten years. Donald McGavran began working on principles of receptivity in India and published The Bridges of God in 1955. *Understanding Church Growth*, first published in 1970 and revised in 1980, developed the concepts further. He was followed by Edward Dayton's Resistance—Receptivity Scale. Peter Wagner began making application of the concepts in the 1970s and 1980s, using Dayton's scale.

Yamamori's Openness Index is another tool developed to further aid our thinking about receptivity of people groups and assist missionaries in cataloging receptivity levels of different groups. Yamamori's premise is that the new focus for missions should be on the 5310 identified unreached people groups, presumably starting with those who rate highest on the four factors in his Openness Index. I would agree. More work like this needs to be done, and further tools must be developed. The following chapter will introduce some of the tools I have developed to help missionaries think about and measure receptivity.

Chapter

Applying Receptivity Principles

Donald McGavran advocates "holding unreceptive peoples lightly." (McGavran 1980:262) In McGavran's view, mission agencies should deploy minimum numbers of missionaries to unreceptive fields and send the most missionaries to the harvest. With observing/sowing agents in place in unreceptive fields, mission personnel work primarily among receptive people groups wait for God to move other groups toward harvest, praying for them that they will become receptive. When they do, more missionaries and resources can be deployed to reach them. Such a mission agency policy harmonizes with Jesus departure command in Matthew 10:14.

With the new tools being developed, and with modern technology and communication, it is possible to chart the receptivity of the world's unreached people groups with a very high degree of accuracy. Missionaries should be trained in the use of these tools and be comfortable using available technologies, information and their own observations to help them monitor the world's people groups.

Missionaries who are already on the field will generally know the people they work with. With little training in receptivity principles, they can make accurate analysis. New missionaries could be trained and deployed to new people groups with instructions to analyze receptivity and be prepared at some point to make the necessary decisions to produce greater fruit for the glory of God.

Combining elements from McGavran's, Dayton and Fraser's, and Yamamori's work on receptivity, with my own thoughts, I have developed what I call the *Receptivity Measurement Index* (see Appendix One for samples) which seeks to analyze and integrate data from social, demographic, economic, political, and religious spheres. It focuses on a particular people group and seeks to ascertain that group's degree of receptivity to the Christian message. The *Receptivity Measurement Index* analyzes eight conditions in the people group, rating each according to two variables, <u>Time Span</u> and <u>Intensity</u>, on a scale of one to ten. The eight conditions are as follows:

   1. *New Immigrants/Arrivals.* This condition deals with the migration of people groups, whether forced by war or environmental conditions or because of economic or other inducements.

2. *Conquered People.* This condition measures how war has affected a people, particularly focusing upon those who were defeated or victimized by war.

3. *Cataclysmic Events.* This condition measures the effects of epidemics, famine, and other natural disasters on a particular people.

4. *Oppressed Minority.* This condition measures how minority status in the area in which a people lives is affecting the group, in terms of the majority's oppressive policies, neglect, control, or other attitudes.

5. *Economic Despair.* This condition measures the level of difficulty a people experiences due to economic factors.

6. *Religious Tolerance.* This condition measures a people group's attitude toward and openness to other religious beliefs, particularly Christianity, either in terms of interest in or acceptance of other points of view.

7. *Political Openness.* This condition corresponds to Yamamori's "Hospitality Index" and measures the official government policy towards outsiders, particularly Christian missionaries, in the country in which the people group lives.

8. *Spiritual Warfare Breakthrough.* This condition, the most subjective, measures the degree to which the forces of prayer and spiritual warfare have succeeded in breaking down spiritual and demonic barriers to reaching the people group.

GO TO THE RIPE FIELDS FIRST!

To use the Receptivity Measurement Index, a number from 0-10 must be indicated in the columns for the two variables, Time Span and Intensity. The two variables are defined as:

1. Time Span uses a scale of 0-10 with 10 indicating that the condition exists in the present. A zero (0) indicates that the condition never existed. A 2 indicates that the condition existed in the distant past and is therefore relatively insignificant to the people's present condition. An 8 indicates that the condition existed in the recent past and is therefore still strongly remembered, and so forth.

2. Intensity uses a scale of 0-10 with 10 indicating the greatest intensity of the condition, meaning the condition is strongly affecting the people. A zero (0) indicates that the condition never existed. A 2 indicates the least intensity of the condition, meaning it is relatively minor or is insignificantly affecting the people. An 8 indicates that the condition is less intense but still strong, and so forth.

For example, on the "New Immigrant/Arrival" condition, those people groups who have never migrated would be a zero (0) on the Time Span variable and a zero (0) on the Intensity variable. The same would be true for the "Conquered Peoples" condition, if they were never conquered in war. "Oppressed Minority" condition would be calculated as to percentage of their population compared with the majority and the degree of oppression, control or neglect they experience from the majority. If they are not a minority people and never have been, they would be a zero (0) on both scales. On the "Political Openness" condition a zero (0) on the Time Span index would show that the particular people group has never been open for missionary activity as an official policy of the country in which they live. A 10 would show that the country is presently open. Numbers 9-1 would indicate how far back in the past since the country was open.

The Intensity index for "Political Openness" would measure the degree of the people group's government's openness, zero (0) being very closed and 10 being very hospitable. The "Spiritual Warfare Breakthrough" condition is the most subjective, because it deals with invisible forces and spiritual conditions such as demonic bondage and the work of the Holy Spirit. A zero (0) on the Time Span variable indicates a breakthrough in the distant past, but none that is detectable in the present. A zero (0) on the Intensity variable indicates no perceivable breakthrough in the people group, while a 10 indicates a breakthrough of revolutionary proportions.

Implied in the use of these two scales are two important rules: (1) The more time that passes after the peak of a condition, the less receptive a people will be. (2) The greater intensity of the condition the longer the people will remain receptive. Both of these rules are analogous to the harvest principles of timeliness and urgency. In other words, the harvest can be lost by delay.

In Appendix One, along with the Receptivity Measurement Index worksheet, there are two samples to illustrate how the Index is used. Our ministry worked with the Indian Tamils in Sri Lanka for more than ten years. The sample sheet is my evaluation of their receptivity based upon my observations and knowledge of the local conditions. Where I was not very sure and had only limited knowledge, I chose the number 5, at the medium of the variable. The same is true for the sample sheet for Thailand, but for the most part I had at least a cursory knowledge of the situation in each category.

McGavran defines a receptive people by the observation that among them "individuals, families, and chains of families" come to faith in Jesus Christ, and by "churches being formed" among that particular people group.

The biggest problem I have had in applying this and other receptivity tools is the absence of a standard. No one has established a baseline or reference point to making receptivity evaluation decisions. For example, when measuring receptivity in a given people group, questions immediately arise: How many people must come to faith in Jesus Christ in one year or one decade for us to confidently say that this people group is "moderately" or "highly" receptive? If a people group is "moderately receptive" how many of their number have believed or will believe? If they are "highly receptive" how many have believed or will believe and how many churches will be planted among them?

In other words, is it possible (or even appropriate?) to establish a minimum standard? If x number of people are converted, and y number of churches are planted, in a given period of time, then this people group could be considered receptive. For obvious reasons, this is shaky ground. Only the Lord of the Harvest can truly make the ultimate judgment about the numbers of conversions. However, such thinking is worthy of our cautious attention as we seek to be obedient workers and be fruitful in harvest work. People are valuable and therefore should be counted! The New Testament record consistently counted new believers, usually listing them in the thousands! Faithfulness to our task today compels us to count as well, and measure what God is doing.

I attempt to answer the question of numbers in a chart I have developed called the *Receptivity: Minimum Harvest Standards* (see Appendix Two).

The *Minimum Harvest Standards* Chart suggests, in a ten year period, the total minimum number of new converts that could be won, the total number of families they would represent, and the total minimum number of new churches that could be planted when evangelizing highly receptive (H) and moderately receptive (M) people groups. This standard is basically structured to be used by an individual missionary in one locale, rather than for broad-based analysis over an entire nation or people. My rationale for localizing receptivity analysis using the MHS Chart is based primarily upon the way people become Christians and make decisions to join the church. These decisions are personal and can also be family decisions (what McGavran calls multi-individual—mutually interdependent decisions), but they cannot be national or even regional. Therefore any studies about conversion trends and receptivity must reflect observations at a local level, even when conversion is happening over an apparently wide area.

The chart could be used for broad analysis, but the minimums would have to be changed, and the study would have to be done by a team of missionaries. These minimums are my estimation of the results an individual missionary or a small team of workers could expect to achieve when working with highly receptive and/or moderately receptive people groups over a number of years.

I am aware of the danger of setting these kinds of standards. But I submit these thoughts as a proto-type for discussion and field experimentation as we seek to be faithful to God in working in His harvest fields. In every harvest the workers give account to the landowner for the amount and quality of grain that is brought in. The "Lord of the Harvest" expects this from his workers. The analogy suggests we have a responsibility to prepare our accounts—in terms of quality and quantity—for the Lord of the Harvest. Is it not then prudent that we think about what He might be expecting from us in those terms?

One important note: The Minimum Harvest Standards Chart assumes that correct methods have been employed to reach these minimums. This is especially true for work among moderately receptive people groups, where right methods are more crucial. If poor methods are used, especially among moderately receptive people groups, the minimum harvest standard could go unattained, even though they were in fact reachable.

GO TO THE RIPE FIELDS FIRST!

The chart implies that harvesting numbers that are below the suggested minimum harvest standards indicates that the work is being done among indifferent, moderately unreceptive, or highly unreceptive people. In such cases, where the minimums are not reached, transferal to a new field should be considered.

I included the column on families because whenever we truly think of people in groups and try to reach them in their native communities, inevitably this will include the nuclear family coming to faith. Counting progress by family units as well as by individuals is a good missiological practice anyway. I chose five persons as a basic family unit, but this number can vary tremendously from culture to culture, depending on how many children a married couple normally has and how many extended family members are an inherent part of the unit. For most cultures, five is probably a minimum number rather than an average.

As I said, these are only preliminary suggestions, a proto-type or working model. More work must be done, both in terms of identifying receptive peoples and in setting minimum harvest standards. I hope these suggestions can stimulate more thoughtful work on the subject.

Again, I realize that making a chart that suggests a "minimum harvest standard" may be offensive to some. But I also suspect that those who are most offended will be veteran missionaries who are either working on unreceptive fields, where the minimums simply cannot be met or they have not found effective methods to reach moderately receptive people.

GO TO THE RIPE FIELDS FIRST!

Missionaries who are working on receptive fields where many are being saved, sometimes far more than my suggested minimums within shorter periods of time, will probably ask why the chart was not more ambitious.

Missionaries on receptive fields are not the problem. The problem lies primarily in our sometimes stubborn human nature. It is a travesty of the Great Commission to remain on unreceptive fields, accepting negligible fruit from our labors year and year, and then to complain when someone suggests that we should move on, or at least try another strategy. I take issue with those who claim that Christian witness in fruitless fields is somehow more noble and indicates a greater degree of faithfulness and sacrifice compared to those who are working fruitfully in harvest fields.

Picturing the analogy in my mind, I can't imagine the Lord of the harvest looking over His fields and smiling with approval as most of His workers are trying to bring in a harvest in fields that are not yet ripe while neighboring fields are ripe yet left to spoil because no one will work there! God's Commission, and our time and His resources, are simply not to be wasted by workers laboring on fields that are not ready for harvest or using programs that are not producing fruit. If some are offended by the suggestion that their labor is being wasted, so be it! Maybe the offense will provoke such workers to more prayer and reflection about what the Lord of harvest expects from them and their labors.

With all the current interest in reaching unreached people groups, more tools should be developed to identify receptive peoples. Further investigations, surveys and strategy development work should be done. A list of people groups and nations that are currently highly receptive should be compiled. The following is a suggested strategy:

1. Research available statistics and demographics, continent by continent and country by country, people by people, to identify unreached, receptive peoples.

2. Using the *Receptivity Measurement Index*, attempt to determine receptivity of potential highly receptive and moderately receptive people groups.

3. Evaluate and analyze evangelism techniques that might be effective in communicating the Gospel and persuading a target receptive people to follow Jesus Christ and become members of His Church.

4. Locate and join hands if possible with nearby national Christians who have a compatible vision to reach the target unreached, receptive people.

5. Deploy a missionary task force to begin a pilot project, planting one or more churches, in one area among the target receptive people.

6. Monitor the progress of the work over a pre-determined time-table, using the *Receptivity: Minimum Harvest Standard* as a guide.

7. If successful, multiply the outreach with additional missionaries and resources toward a reachable goal.

GO TO THE RIPE FIELDS FIRST!

As I said, more work must be done to make increased use of receptivity principles. Of the 5310 unreached people groups in the world at present, it seems essential that world missionary priorities should be focused upon those people groups that are reachable. Accurate ways to identify these people must be found. Re-deployment of the present missionary force and new deployment of more missionaries is imperative in order to harvest where the harvest is ripe and hasten the pace of world evangelization.

The author welcomes your correspondence:

J. Douglas Gehman
President/Director

8590 Highway 98 West
P.O. Box 3040
Pensacola, Florida 32516-3040

Telephone: 850-453-3453
FAX: 850-456-6001

E-Mail: douggehman@gme.org
www.gme.org

About the Author

Doug and his wife Beth Ann were first sent to Asia by their home church in Indiana in 1978. In 1984, they pioneered their own ministry, AsiaNet Ministries, in Sri Lanka and Thailand. The AsiaNet Ministries team conducted open air crusades over much of Sri Lanka and South Thailand and eventually helped plant 30 churches in Sri Lanka's hill country region. The Gehmans spent 15 years living and working in Asia.

Doug attended Goshen College and Fuller Theological Seminary, and earned Master's and Doctorate degrees in Missions at Liberty Christian University.

Doug and Beth became affiliated with Globe Missionary Evangelism in 1987. Globe is an inter-denominational missionary sending agency with over 200 personnel in 35 nations. Doug joined the Globe Staff as Assistant Director in 1994, and became Director in 2001. He now serves as both President and Director of the organization.

Doug and Beth were married in 1976. Together they have ministered to missionaries and churches in over 40 nations. The Gehmans live in Pensacola, Florida. They have four children.

GO TO THE RIPE FIELDS FIRST!

GO TO THE RIPE FIELDS FIRST!

Notes and Sources

Dayton, Edward R. and C. Peter Wagner
To Reach the Unreached: A Report to the Lausanne Committee for World Evangelization,
Willowbank, Bermuda, January 16-20, 1978, p. 9.
Note: This paper charts several receptive and resistant people groups in different parts of the world on the R./R axis.

Dayton, Edward R. and Fraser, David A.
Planning Strategies for World Evangelization,
Eerdmans, Grand Rapids; MARC Monrovia, CA 1990.

Jamieson, Fausset & Brown
Commentary on the Whole Bible,
Zondervan Publishing House, Grand Rapids, MI 1961.

Johnstone, Patrick
Operation World, 5th Edition,
Zondervan, Grand Rapids, MI 1993.

McGavran, Donald A.
Understanding Church Growth, Fully Revised.
William B. Eerdmans, Grand Rapids, MI 1980.

McGavran, Donald A.
The Bridges of God,
Friendship Press, New York 1955.

Wagner, C. Peter
Strategies for Church Growth,
Regal Books, Ventura, CA 1987.

Winter, Ralph D.
Perspectives on the World Christian Movement, A Reader Revised Edition,
William Carey Library, Pasadena, CA 1992.

Yamamori, Tetsunao
Penetrating Missions' Final Frontier,
Intervarsity Press, Downers Grove, Illinois 1993.

GO TO THE RIPE FIELDS FIRST!

Appendix One

RECEPTIVITY MEASUREMENT INDEX

People Group: _____

CONDITION	TIME SPAN	INTENSITY
1. New Immigrants/ Arrivals		
2. Conquered Peoples		
3. Cataclysmic Events		
4. Oppressed Minority		
5. Economic Despair		
6. Religious Tolerance		
7. Political Openness		
8. Spiritual Warfare Breakthrough		
TOTALS		

Receptivity Measurement: _____

Key:	110-140	Highly Receptive
	70-109	Moderately Receptive
	50-69	Indifferent
	30-49	Moderately Resistant
	14-29	Highly Resistant

® 2004 J. Douglas Gehman

GO TO THE RIPE FIELDS FIRST!

RECEPTIVITY MEASUREMENT INDEX

People Group: Thailand Ethnic Thais

CONDITION	TIME SPAN	INTENSITY
1. New Immigrants/ Arrivals	0	0
2. Conquered Peoples	2	2
3. Cataclysmic Events	3	3
4. Oppressed Minority	0	0
5. Economic Despair	2	2
6. Religious Tolerance	5	5
7. Political Openness	7	7
8. Spiritual Warfare Breakthrough	3	3
TOTALS	**22**	**22**

Receptivity Measurement: 44 – Moderately Resistant

Key:	110-140	Highly Receptive
	70-109	Moderately Receptive
	50-69	Indifferent
	30-49	Moderately Resistant
	14-29	Highly Resistant

® 2004 J. Douglas Gehman

GO TO THE RIPE FIELDS FIRST!

RECEPTIVITY MEASUREMENT INDEX

People Group: Sri Lanka Indian Tamils

CONDITION	TIME SPAN	INTENSITY
1. New Immigrants/ Arrivals	5	5
2. Conquered Peoples	5	5
3. Cataclysmic Events	0	0
4. Oppressed Minority	9	7
5. Economic Despair	9	9
6. Religious Tolerance	7	7
7. Political Openness	2	3
8. Spiritual Warfare Breakthrough	5	5
TOTALS	**42**	**41**

Receptivity Measurement: 83 – Moderately Receptive

Key:	110-140	Highly Receptive
	70-109	Moderately Receptive
	50-69	Indifferent
	30-49	Moderately Resistant
	14-29	Highly Resistant

® 2004 J. Douglas Gehman

Appendix Two

RECEPTIVITY

MINIMUM HARVEST STANDARDS

YEAR	Total Adherents M/H	Total Families M/H	Total Churches M/H
1	25/50	5/10	1 / 1
2	50/100	10/20	1 / 1
3	75/200	15/40	1 / 2
4	100/400	20/80	1 / 4
5	150/600	30/120	2 / 6
6	250/1000	50/200	3 / 10
7	400/1500	80/300	4 / 15
8	500/2000	100/400	5 / 18
9	750/2500	150/500	7 / 20
10	1000/3000	200/600	10 / 25

Key:

M - Estimated amount for a moderately receptive people

H - Estimated amount for a highly receptive people

GO TO THE RIPE FIELDS FIRST!

Order Form For:

Go To The *Ripe Fields* First!

Please print clearly.

Name: _____

Address: _____

City: _____

State: _____ Zip: _____

Telephone: _____

Email: _____

_____ copies of book @ $8.00 each $_____

Postage and handling @ $1.50 per book $_____

Total amount enclosed $_____

Make checks payable to:

Globe Publishing
P.O. Box 3040
Pensacola, FL 32516

Telephone orders: 850.453.3453
Website orders: www.gme.org
(most major credit cards accepted)